The Big Green Poetry Machine

West Midlands
Edited by Annabel Cook

First published in Great Britain in 2008 by:
Young Writers
Remus House
Coltsfoot Drive
Peterborough
PE2 9JX
Telephone: 01733 890066
Website: www.youngwriters.co.uk

All Rights Reserved

© Copyright Contributors *2008*

SB ISBN 978-1 84413 724 0

Foreword

Young Writers' Big Green Poetry Machine is a showcase for our nation's most brilliant young poets to share their thoughts, hopes and fears for the planet they call home.

Young Writers was established in 1991 to nurture creativity in our children and young adults, to give them an interest in poetry and an outlet to express themselves. Seeing their work in print will encourage them to keep writing as they grow, and become our poets of tomorrow.

Selecting the poems has been challenging and immensely rewarding. The effort and imagination invested by these young writers makes their poems a pleasure to enjoy reading time and time again.

Contents

Berkswell CE Primary School
Cathy Parker (9)	1
Callum Parker (11)	2
Charlotte Harvey (9)	3
Isabella Fowler (9)	3
Katie Holmes (10)	4
Rachel Field (10)	5
Eleanor Holmes (8)	5
Matilda Lamberts (10)	6
Eloise Stevens (8)	6
Teqeela Uppal (8)	7
Joanna Porter (8)	7
Rhyannon Cariad Jones (8)	8
Emily Bailey (9)	8
Lily Jones (10)	9
Amy Hancox (8)	9
James Goodwin (8)	9

Binley Woods Primary School
Oliver Rowles-Bourne (11)	10
Sean Dowsing (10)	10
Alice Phillips (11)	11
Ellie Jones (11)	11
Brooke Brogden (11)	12
Emilia Sorrill (11)	12
Sally Thomson (11)	13
Abdul-Waseh Afghan (11)	13
Alex Griffin (11)	14
Zac Mortlock (11)	14
Jack Cooksley (11)	14
Leah Payne (11)	15

Corpus Christi Catholic Primary School
Diana Canterbury (10)	15
Billy Moore (10)	16
Kiera Taylor (9)	16
Alix Mace (10)	17
Callum Differ (10)	17
Aric Purcell (10)	18

Amy Loonam (10)   18
Lachlan Elliott (10)   19

East Park Junior School
Jak Evans (11)   19
Jarad Tansley (11)   20
Shaneaqua Edwards (11)   20
Danielle Evans (11)   21
Amy Grigg (11)   21
Benjamin Alexander Byrne (11)   22
Ben Howell (10)   22
Adam Nightingale (11)   23
Leanne Smith (11)   23
Jamieleigh Ikin (10)   24
Shannon Watkiss (11)   24
Charlotte Poole (11)   25
Nathaniel Wilson (11)   25
Gurjant Buttar (11)   26
Sophie Dhanoa (11)   26
Abbie Tolley (11)   26
Shelby Freeman (10)   27
Savannah Wilkinson (11)   27
Amanda Bird (11)   27
Cameron Jones (10)   28
Chloe Lewis (11)   28
Amy Lewis (11)   29
Kayleigh Hill (11)   29
Ashleigh Pilsbury (11)   30
Sarah Louise Bagshaw (11)   30
Kay Ann Allen (10)   30
Charlie Crawford (11)   31
Emma White (11)   31
Dionne Sherelle Abrahams (11)   31
Danny Homer (11)   32

Fallings Park Primary School
Brandon Parker (11)   32
Amy Newton (11)   33
Daniel Faulkner (11)   33
Jessie Ansell (11)   34
Ravan Chahal Singh (9)   34

Taylor Jefimik (11) — 35
Taneesha Lewis (9) — 35
Sonia Puri (9) — 36
Courtney Haynes (10) — 36

Four Oaks Primary School
Harry Chiam (10) — 37
Georgia Davies Winkless (11) — 37
Emma Hogg (11) — 38
Courtney Jones (11) — 38
Rebecca Cooper (11) — 39
Benjamin Knowles (11) — 39
Beth Woodward (11) — 40
George Brayford (11) — 40

Hearsall Community Primary School
Safiyah Iqbal (11) — 41
Kiana Richardson (10) — 41
Phoebe May Emerson (11) — 42
Dineo Masiane (10) — 42
Connor Young (11) — 43
Zanele Mhlanga (11) — 43
Abdullah Khan (11) — 44
Keisha Hibbert (11) — 44
Ross Jordan Hatt (11) — 44

Lyndon Green Junior School
Jonathan Faulkner (8) — 45
Amy Nicholas (8) — 45
Reece Wyatt (8) — 45
Joshua Beer (8) — 46
Grace Tavner (7) — 46
Darcie Brady (7) — 47
Aiden Everett (8) — 47
Amy-Leigh Tuffield (8) — 48
Rebecca Lily Sumner (7) — 48
Zack Yeomans (7) — 49
Ryan Thomas (8) — 49
Emma Louise Hanson (7) — 50
Maisy Dewell (8) — 50
Jessica Jane Milner (7) — 51

Abigail Finnegan (8)	51
Callum Rose (8)	52
Poppy Goddard (8)	52
Alisha Haria (8)	53
Christopher Jackson (8)	53
Tori Leah Southall (7)	54
Nialls Harry Neville Whyley (8)	54
James Burnham (8)	55

Roman Way First School

Amie Woodward (9)	55
Siana Diane Beard (7)	56
Jade Hunt (8)	56
Charlie William Harris (7)	56
Catie Williamson (9)	57
Ciera Browne (7)	57
Rachel Govada (8)	57
Zoe Louise Nicholls (9)	58
Liam Holmes (8)	58
Mollie Goode (9)	58

St Francis CE Primary School, Bournville

Gemma May Alice Sealey (11)	59
Dominic Glynn (11)	59
Joseph Smith (10)	59
Joshua Palmer (11)	60
Daniel Bagby (11)	60
Naomi Powell (10)	61
Harry Cullotty (11)	61
Tazmin Vandriwala (11)	62
Zoë Harrison (11)	62
Angus Smith (11)	63
Emily Jean Bullivant (11)	63
Rebecca Guy (11)	64
Michael Lennox (11)	64
Anaya Bolar (11)	65
Nathan Rees (11)	65
Jamie Tennant (11)	65
Kallum O'Toole (11)	66

St Peter's Catholic First School, Bromsgrove
Charlotte Lowe (8)	66
Briony Read (8)	67
Niamh Caffrey (9)	67
Chloe-Ann Rooney (9)	68
Joseph Smith (8)	68
Holly Robinson (8)	69
Katie Burke (8)	69
Rebecca Macpherson (9)	70
Eden Peppercorn (9)	70
Rhiannon Edwards (8)	71

Woodhouse Primary School
Hanad Arwo (10)	71
Muhammad Zeeshan Sartaj (9)	72
Bradley Walton (10)	72
Gurjeevan Chal (10)	73
Jay Copper (10)	73
William Howes (11)	74
Lily-May Miller (9)	74
Elizabeth Jane Thorpe (9)	75
Irish Winkelmann (8)	75
Nathan White (10)	76
Mathew Riddle (9)	76
Létitia Treacy (9)	77
Luke Houghton (9)	77
Sophie Burrows (9)	78
Jasmin Tantoco (7)	78
Holung Lee (8)	78
Pariese Paul (7)	79
Casey Miller (8)	79
Ákos Szücs (10)	79
Hadis Mohamadi (8)	80
Charlotte Smith (9)	80
Meghana Vaidya (9)	81
Sara Elsharif (9)	81
Courtney Bonehill (8)	82
Cameron Hadley (9)	82
Shannon Byrne (9)	82
Christian Lewis Bell (8)	83
Mia Shannon (8)	83

Hema Chumber (7) 83
Amardeep Chal (8) 84
Anisah Shabir (8) 84
Prashant Ramnatsing (8) 84
Tahmid Kalam (8) 85
Ellie Louise Shannon (8) 85
Reece Taylor (7) 85

Woodlands Primary School
Holly Edwards (9) 86
Charlotte Maija Johnson-Howe (9) 86
Emma Campbell (9) 87
Amy Hampshire (11) 87
Lucy Stirling (8) 88
Megan Hampshire (9) 88
Hannah Bullows (8) 89
Laura Carless (11) 89
Emily Spittle (10) 90
Alan Melling (11) 90
Victoria Bird (9) 91
Joshua Pullinger (9) 91
Joseph Turton (8) 92
Jaye Roberts (8) 92
Sam Bradley (9) 92
Megan Annie Clayton (9) 93
Lucy Emma Ball (9) 93
Chloe Freeman-Chick (9) 93
Demi-Leigh Hems (8) 94
Brooke Holland (7) 94
Sophie Hampshire (8) 94
Jessica Lockley (9) 95
Chloe Babiy (9) 95
Millie Slater (10) 95
Leia Walker (8) 96
Abigail Whistance (7) 96
Rachael Burgess (10) 97
Emily Watton (8) 97
Sophie Green (8) 98
Nathan Reeves (8) 98
Kelsey Bentley (10) 99
Sophie Ann Thorpe Gogerty (9) 99

Ellie Valerie Dobell (10)	100
Jordan Saunders	100
Charlotte Spink (10)	101
Samuel Parkes (10)	101
Shân Jones (10)	102
Emma Garley (10)	102
Hollie Jones (9)	103
William Davis (10)	103
Holly Crook (10)	104
Patrick Patton (9)	104
Callum Lewis Street (10)	105
Paris Mai Lawrence (10)	105
Adam Walters (10)	106
Rebecca Mills (10)	106
Leah Wilkinson (10)	106
Bethany Haddon (10)	107
Sophie Richards (10)	107
Abbie Chester (10)	107
Max Rushton (10)	108
Nathan Miles (10)	108
Millie Clarke (9)	108

The Poems

Let's Look After Our World

Animals these days just come and go
To this tragic decline we must say no.
The forests are cut down and then left to burn
Leaving the animals with nowhere to turn.

Today the dolphins may drive through the waves
But in a few years they will be in their graves.
Fishing nets drown them and pull them below the sea
We must alter the fishing nets and let dolphins swim free.

The eastern gorilla is a gentle giant
Regarding the preservation of their forests we must be defiant.
The old man of the forest means orang-utan
Save the forest and you will save this old man.

Giant pandas are still under threat
The destruction of their habitat is not sorted yet.
You may think they are sweet so make that thought last
For tomorrow they may be a thing of the past!

Global warming is happening so quick
Stopping this happen now, that's the trick.
The ice caps are melting, that we do know
The polar bears have noticed, there's a lot less snow!

So please sit down and have a think
All these animals could become extinct.
We must act now and make things right
To save the animals we should always fight.

Cathy Parker (9)
Berkswell CE Primary School

Reinforcing The Rainforests

You wonder, what is a rainforest?
I bet you would love to know.
A place where loads of animals roam
And where plants live and grow.

The trees are now all being cut
Soon only nine percent will remain.
What have we done to our beautiful world?
We must be completely insane.

It really could be a fantastic world
If you just looked after it a little bit more.
There'd be monkeys and snakes and frogs too
It would be animals galore.

All of the animals live in the forest
Probably over one million kinds
When the green trees grow so do they
So don't act as if you're blind.

We need the green trees for oxygen
Because rainforest population live there too.
Rainforests provide paper we need although
We need to save our animals; we need to think this through.

Rainforest are where the animals thrive
They live there, yes they do.
They are all so wonderful and pretty
It really is quite true.

So please sit down and think a while
How amazing these rainforests really are.
They help sustain our environment with no help from human kind
We can save our world by helping them, let's hope we get that far.

Callum Parker (11)
Berkswell CE Primary School

Don't Let The Animals Go

Our world is melting away because of us
They'll be gone completely
But we know in our hearts we want them to stay.
Global warming will come but it's not game over yet,
Surely you still want a tiger as a pet.
To tiger cubs their lives are like a fog
Next, extinction for the poor golden frog.
Both these creatures will no longer be new.
They will be extinct all because of you.
Global warming will come, don't blame me, blame everyone.
Cute polar bears you go, aah, cute
But never stop to think soon they'll be extinct.
Thirty years from now they may not wake up to a brand new day
All because of you!
I know you want them to stay.

Charlotte Harvey (9)
Berkswell CE Primary School

The Mountain Gorilla Project

The mountain gorilla project is a go
Gorillas rushing around to and fro,
Taking the species to a safer place
Uniting them to nature in its amazing grace.
Surrounded by trees being cut down
Sold for a certain fee giving the gorillas a frown.
The Rwanda Trust office running a project
Using very safe gorilla friendly objects.
Never giving up trying to save these creatures
Hoping not to harm their beautiful features.
Its fur so soft, smooth and hairy
Making people think that they aren't scary.
So if you see a mountain gorilla trudging along
Think before you kill them, *bang* and they're gone!

Isabella Fowler (9)
Berkswell CE Primary School

My Grandpa And The Orang-Utan

My grandpa has an orang-utan,
Living in his house.
It really is a weird pet,
I wish he had a mouse.

One snowy day my grandpa,
Came home early from work.
To find his Tanya orang-utan,
Acting like a berk.

My grandpa screamed and shouted,
The whole street could hear the bungle.
He threatened his orang-utan,
About sending her back to the jungle.

So Tanya packed her bags
And left for the jungle next day.
But when she got there,
She didn't know what to say.

Her friends, family and home
Were no longer there.
So my grandpa's young friend Tanya
Could only stop and stare.

The loggers had been
And felled all the trees.
Now palm oil plants
Swayed in the breeze.

So my grandpa still has an orang-utan
Living in his house.
It really is a weird pet,
I'm glad it's not a mouse.

Katie Holmes (10)
Berkswell CE Primary School

Muddy Mountain Gorillas

I'm peaceful and relaxed
Though I might need to get waxed
I spend a lot of time looking for food
And I have a very happy mood.
When I was a baby I was covered in black hair
My mum gave me tender loving care.
My mum gave me lots of attention
Swinging, playing and getting a detention.
My dad is very scary
But he is a bit hairy.
He beats his chest and bares his teeth
When his friend dies he is full of grief.
I am a vegetarian, my favourite food is berries
Though I don't particularly like jellies.
Nettles and leaves are next in line
There wouldn't be any of those in a mine.

Rachel Field (10)
Berkswell CE Primary School

Bumblebees

What would we do without bumblebees?
There would be no flowers or trees.
There would be no pollen for honey,
Do you think that would be funny?

Why are bees becoming extinct?
The farmers cut all the hedges down,
But bees do not like to go to town.
So put some flowers in your garden
And build some bumblebee homes.
Let's help these stripy buzzing creatures
Stay in their honeycombs.

Eleanor Holmes (8)
Berkswell CE Primary School

Bye Mum

So small, so sweet!
I adore eating shoots,
Can you be my best friend?
I will cuddle you morning till end.
My mum was taken away
To do circus acts and plays.
She was taken away when I was in bed
I don't know if she's alive or dead.
My mum was so unbelievably pretty
Now she's gone, it's such a pity.
But I will be like her one day
When I grow up I will be beautiful, *hooray!*
Can you guess what I am?
Of course, I am an orang-utan!

Matilda Lamberts (10)
Berkswell CE Primary School

Koalas Under Threat

K oalas are killed every day
O ur homes are being knocked down
A ll our food is disappearing
L ife is tough in the bush
A ustralia's favourite animal is the koala
S ave the koala.

Eloise Stevens (8)
Berkswell CE Primary School

Chimpanzee

C aring for them is a full time job
H elp them now and stop this cruelty
I' m very sad, how do you feel?
M y love for them will never fade
P eople killing, why, why, why?
A shtrays made from their hands
N ever give their enemies a hand
Z oos are not for chimpanzees
E nemies are enemies don't you know
E at your words and don't let them go!

Teqeela Uppal (8)
Berkswell CE Primary School

Jaguars

J aguars are under threat
A ll our homes are being knocked down
G uns are killing us for making coats
U nder trees we try to hide
A merica is not a great place for jaguars
R are animals we are getting
S ave our jaguars.

Joanna Porter (8)
Berkswell CE Primary School

Don't Let The Tigers Go

Don't let the tigers go
It's really cruel don't you know
Their beautiful skin being ripped away
About twenty every day,
The little cubs playing in the sun
Chasing birds, having fun.
Their glinting teeth in the moonlight
Look at their eyes; they're so beautiful and so bright.
Licking their paws keeping themselves clean
When they're hunting they can be mean.
Their furry golden skin like honey
Some people buying their coats for money.
Some people ripping down their habitats
Sometimes using their skins for mats.
Look at the tigers, look and enjoy
Only a little love you have to employ.
Problems like this are so very blue
And it could be all because of you!

Rhyannon Cariad Jones (8)
Berkswell CE Primary School

Don't Let Chimpanzees Go

C himpanzees are becoming extinct
H elp them stay alive
I really want them to stay alive
M ost threatened is the Nigerian chimpanzee
P oachers go and hunt chimpanzees for meat
A ll chimpanzees are becoming extinct
N o, don't let them become extinct
Z oos are cruel
E ncourage people to help them stay in the forest
E ndangered they shouldn't be.

Emily Bailey (9)
Berkswell CE Primary School

Silly Spectacle Bears

Spectacle bears never really care, they like lots of milk
Then eventually their fur turns to silk.
They are sweet and harmless but boy do they smell!
They are very special because they are South America's only bear
                                    and they have plenty of hair.
They can bite through plants with ease but aren't too keen on peas.
When they are small they are cute and cuddly then they get
                                    fat and muddy.
When they are twelve, the best, they can eat and rest.
They wrinkle their noses and pull silly poses, that's because
                                    they're spectacle bears.

Lily Jones (10)
Berkswell CE Primary School

Poor Pandas

P anda food is dying quickly because of climate change
A nd did you know there are only sixteen hundred left in the world
N obody really cares for pandas anymore
D eforestation between 1947 and 1989, the habitat of pandas shrank by half
A nd it's our world being killed and it's our fault!

Amy Hancox (8)
Berkswell CE Primary School

Cod Fish

C od fish are under threat because of fishermen
O ver one thousand cod fish are dead every year
D o not throw dead fish back into the sea.

James Goodwin (8)
Berkswell CE Primary School

Global Warming

G reenhouse gas
L ife changing
O ut in space
B eware the atmosphere's breaking
A nywhere in the world
L ives are ruining

W hy do it?
A lways you'll hear people saying
R emember the good times
M aybe make new
I' ve already done my bit
N ow it's your turn too
G o on, now you do it!

Oliver Rowles-Bourne (11)
Binley Woods Primary School

Think!

Think to yourself,
Stop fighting and think,
Why fight? It's bad,
So just stop
Because war is lethal.
People will die,
So think to yourself
And *stop!*

Sean Dowsing (10)
Binley Woods Primary School

Water

Drip, drip, drop, drop
Water falling, water falling.
Brushing teeth, washing hands,
Water falling, water falling.
Having baths, having drinks,
Water falling, water falling.
Drip, drip, drop, drop,
Water falling, water falling.
The tap is on,
Turn it off!
Water falling, water falling.
The tap is off,
Don't leave it on!

Alice Phillips (11)
Binley Woods Primary School

Why Do We Need War?

I heard a bomb this morning
I think my time is dawning.
I listen in the night
I sit up waiting for the light.
Nobody really cares about me
Why can't they just see?
Everybody thinks we're safe
But is there a safe place?

Ellie Jones (11)
Binley Woods Primary School

Fighting And War

War is horrible and also bad
War makes people upset
War makes people sad.

People get horribly injured, possibly even killed.
People who fight are killing the world.
People's hearts will have to be refilled.

Will people ever learn?
Who really knows?
Everyone has some concern
Your feeling really shows.

Brooke Brogden (11)
Binley Woods Primary School

Water

Drip, drip, drip,
The tap's on at the sink.
Drop, drop, drop,
Turn the tap off!
You need water for many things
Cleaning your teeth and washing your face
Taking a bath and watering the plants.
You also have water to drink
So when you use water you need to think!

Emilia Sorrill (11)
Binley Woods Primary School

Homeless

We have homes
Some do not.
We have food
Some do not.
We have toys
Some do not.
We sleep in beds
Some do not.
We are happy
Some are not.
We should be grateful for what we have got.
So next time you say it's not fair
Think!

Sally Thomson (11)
Binley Woods Primary School

Water

Don't waste water in our nation
Think about our next generation.
In Africa they don't even have a sink
But we have masses to drink.
Turn the shower on, not the bath
Then you'll find that you've saved half.
In Africa it's hard to find
So why don't you use your mind?

Abdul-Waseh Afghan (11)
Binley Woods Primary School

Why Be Racist?

Black or white
We're all the same,
It's just a colour
No one's to blame.
When you bully someone else
What if that person was yourself?
Would you like it
I really doubt it
After all,
It's just a colour.

Alex Griffin (11)
Binley Woods Primary School

Water

W ater we have got gallons of it
A lthough the people in some countries have none at all
T urn on the shower, don't use the bath
E verlasting water, there's no such thing to
R educe is important, so save water now.

Zac Mortlock (11)
Binley Woods Primary School

Water

W ater is something precious
A re you wasting it?
T hink about people who don't have water
E veryone should have it
R espect the fact that we have water, let's use it wisely.

Jack Cooksley (11)
Binley Woods Primary School

Wildlife

W e need to help the animals
I f we don't they will not survive
L ives are hard for the animals
D on't forget to help them
L ife will be a better place
I f you help the animals in our environment
F ind a loving home for the wildlife in our environment
E very day don't forget to help them.

Leah Payne (11)
Binley Woods Primary School

The Big Green World

What's happening to our beautiful planet?
Poverty, war and litter
Why is it all so bitter?
Nothing can change without us.

What's happening to our lovely animals?
Pets in the wild,
They're as important as a child
Nothing can change without us.

We are the children of tomorrow
We *can* help.

Diana Canterbury (10)
Corpus Christi Catholic Primary School

The Race Of Time

The climate is rising
Our future is collapsing.
Racism is now an activity
Friendship is becoming non existent.
Everywhere is littered
Pollution makes me anxious
Extinction is too huge to cope with
Poverty is everywhere.
Climate change is winning the race
The Earth is at its fastest decline.
It makes me sad to know that we are not making an effort
But I'm surely sure, I'm positive that the Earth will win the race.
So as the black flag unfolds the truth the sensation is a roar
But all that I can see now is a very sad draw.
My future is rolling on and everybody's around me
So cheer up now there are smiles all around for we are kids
of the future
We *can* do something, we *can* do it!

Billy Moore (10)
Corpus Christi Catholic Primary School

In The War

It's a terrible sight to see people at war
I jump out of the bed like a bullet and watch out the window
As people just fall to the ground dead
Bang! Bang! It's very hard to live a life in the war.
As the tank goes by I feel myself crying
I close my eyes and pretend I live a normal life
Not in the war, just how it is today.
I want to stay here as long as I live
War is death and death is war.

Kiera Taylor (9)
Corpus Christi Catholic Primary School

What Would We Do Without Animals?

Imagine a world without animals
It seems pretty dull doesn't it?
Nothing to keep as a pet
No company at all.

The miaow of a cat echoing softly
The scratch from a guinea pig, it's harsh
All these animals around
Not to exist at all.

The seas desolate and empty
The jungle you can't hear a roar
Most animals won't exist
Not . . . at . . . all.

No red squirrels to collect nuts
No honeybees to make honey
Oh please, tell me what you'd do
What would we do without animals?

Alix Mace (10)
Corpus Christi Catholic Primary School

War

Bullets flying everywhere
Bombs falling here and there
In their air raid shelter they hide
Hoping for victory on their side
In 1945 they hear
In England, there is a cheer!

Callum Differ (10)
Corpus Christi Catholic Primary School

Let's Stop Things

Let's stop war
Let's stop it for sure.
Let's stop extinction
Let's take some action
Let's stop litter
Let's make this place better.
Let's stop racism
Let's stop sexism
Let's stop climate change
Let's turn the page.

Aric Purcell (10)
Corpus Christi Catholic Primary School

Stop Pollution

As we stroll in the park
We see pollution in the lake
And I ask myself,
Why do we pollute?

Police should stand by the lake
To stop people polluting
The council should put gates up
That would be even better.
Stop pollution!

Amy Loonam (10)
Corpus Christi Catholic Primary School

Help The World

If you don't pollute the sea
Our world, our land will be lovely.
Help the world not with a letter
It is nice but it could be better.
Help it now with a little know how
We hope it's ours forever and ever
Help it now because it's now or never.

Lachlan Elliott (10)
Corpus Christi Catholic Primary School

Save The Polar Bears

P olar bears are so cute
O r do you think different?
L eave our polar bears alone
A nd also save the Earth.
R ound the Earth they live

B ut you can help them too
E xtinction is a problem
A nd if you don't
R oar, they will roar at you
S o save our polar bears.

Jak Evans (11)
East Park Junior School

Extinction

In the jungle will animals die?
Children find out and they will cry.
Nasty humans cut the trees
Breaking others habitats, that is really mean!
Where will they live? Where's the food?
The humans made tigers in a bad mood.

No food, no home, quicker than a snap
Animals die out when you think they're having a nap.
I hate it now, cute animals gone forever
There is no trace, they're not going to reappear.

Jarad Tansley (11)
East Park Junior School

The Rap Of Racism

Racism is wrong and you know it's true
Because there's no difference between me and you.
Black and white are both the same
And people who disagree are madly insane.
If you're a different culture to others you see
Just move on with your life and be who you want to be.
People who are racist should be ashamed
But don't let yourself down by being afraid.
I hope that racism will stop all together
And people who were victims will live happily forever.

Shaneaqua Edwards (11)
East Park Junior School

Polar Bears

P olar bears are dying all over
O ur world is making them extinct
L ittle are still alive
A re you helping pollute the Earth?
R ain doesn't help the icebergs

B ut *you* can help.
E xtinction has become a problem
A re you trying to save our polar bears?
R are, are still alive
S ave our polar bears!

Danielle Evans (11)
East Park Junior School

Recycling Is Good, Litter Is Bad

Recycling is good, litter is bad,
Put rubbish in the bin
So that animals don't get hurt.
Recycling is good, litter is bad,
Stop throwing litter on the floor to help the environment.
Recycling is good, litter is bad,
Just stop throwing litter on the floor
The world will look better.
Recycling is good, litter is bad.

Amy Grigg (11)
East Park Junior School

The Tsunami

The tsunami is coming
In a matter of time
Everyone is running
For their helpless lives.

The tsunami is coming
Everyone is so terrified
It is getting out of hand
I feel so terrified
Not knowing what to do.

The tsunami is coming
I hear the vicious thunder
I feel the tough wind
I see the high seas
I see it coming
The tsunami is here.

It is now here
It is as tall as a skyscraper
As wide as a town
As fast as a cheetah hunting its prey
As tough as a building.

The tsunami is here
I know it is close
All I see is death around me
It is too late to run now
The tsunami is here.

Benjamin Alexander Byrne (11)
East Park Junior School

Homeless

The homeless wear rags for clothes
To hide all of their skinny bones.
Wet and damp their bodies ache
Their arms and legs start to shake.
Now all I've got to offer is a moan and groan.

Ben Howell (10)
East Park Junior School

Unhappy Animals

The lion family bolt happily in the wild,
The bears get killed for their style.
The baby rhinos cry for their mom,
Now the poachers have done.
Rhinos heads on the wall,
The poachers sell stuff on their stall.
Flamingos stand in the sun,
Now they have all gone.
Lizards skitter across the heat,
Tigers roar in a beat.
Dolphins jump out of the sea,
Birds sing in the tree.
Kangaroo jump in the sand,
And the dog gives out his hand.
The cat miaows to the moon,
The guinea pig hides in his room.

Adam Nightingale (11)
East Park Junior School

Stop Litter

S ave the planet
T ogether we can help
O ur planet needs us
P aper and cans can be recycled

L ook after planet Earth
I mprove the world
T ogether we can stop extinction
T he animals have a life too
E verybody stop littering
R ecycle, reuse and reduce.

Leanne Smith (11)
East Park Junior School

Litter

Our world is full of pollution
Because you keep dropping litter
But there's no conclusion
But it is really bitter.
You should stop it now
Because when those trees fall down
You will have to duck down.
I hope you've taken my advice
I hope you stop it now,
Our world is really clean
And know you and me don't need to bow.
Now the sun is out
And you and me can play,
So when your friends drop litter
What will you say?

Jamieleigh Ikin (10)
East Park Junior School

Homelessness

I'm alone, I'm on my own
My tummy gives a strange moan.
I'm alone, I have no home
No safe place to have grown.
I'm alone, the rain is pain
If I wonder I get a cane
I'm alone begging and muddy
Oh my God, I wish I was greedy.
I'm alone needing warmth in the bitter cold
I don't want to grow old.

Shannon Watkiss (11)
East Park Junior School

Healthy Eating

My poem's about healthy eating,
Pick up a banana, that's good for me.
Yum, yum, yum, I want some more
I'll pick an apple from a tree.

Strawberries, apple, grapes and kiwis,
Who likes these fruit, me, me, me!
Carrots, broccoli, peas and sprouts,
You'll be mega healthy, not even a doubt.

I'm mega healthy and it's fun, fun, fun!
I'm gonna live forever.
Eating the right food is really important,
I'll eat the right foods for ever and ever.

Charlotte Poole (11)
East Park Junior School

Starvation

S ad people living in the streets
T he poor lying with no treats
A ble to fight through the thunderous night
R ather die or lie or even fly
V arious people giving them the beady eye
A nnoying little flies
T aking away disease
I n the night
O nly under the light
N othing to do starvation is true.

Nathaniel Wilson (11)
East Park Junior School

Homeless Forever

Homeless people moaning and groaning
Babies and children, suffering from hunger and cold.
I didn't have food I was in a bad mood
Mothers in tears, praying for a miracle.
You can feel the fear out on the road
We don't have to struggle
We take it for granted
We wake up in the morning and know we're safe.

Gurjant Buttar (11)
East Park Junior School

Homeless

Hungry, lonely, cold and withered
People sat as they shuddered and shivered.
An emaciated mother embraced her dead child whilst shedding a tear
She knew she was living in fear.
Living on the street rummaging through bins
As people search for food for their kin.
Torn clothes, sleeping rough
To endure this pain you must be tough.

Sophie Dhanoa (11)
East Park Junior School

Litter Bins

The Earth is polluted
Species are dying and time's running out.
Rubbish is falling, falling like bombs
Even the birds are too sad to sing songs.
Whales are finding it hard to swim
So put your rubbish in the bin!

Abbie Tolley (11)
East Park Junior School

Tsunami

In Thailand 2005, the tsunami hit and not that many people
                                                are still alive.
The tsunami is coming, bolt your doors, hide under your bed
The tsunami is coming; thousands of people are already dead.
The tsunami is coming, countries are destroyed,
This is what the cities tried to avoid.
The tsunami is coming, help those countries, those are in need
Send them aid, please, they plead.

Shelby Freeman (10)
East Park Junior School

Litter

The wind quakes, the litter's swirling all around
As people listen and make not a word or sound.
There's danger to other animals they have lots and lots of fears
In the sea floats bits of litter, discarded by the hand of people
                                                who are bitter.
Litter all over the floor making our Earth a disgrace.
It's everywhere; it's all over the place.

Savannah Wilkinson (11)
East Park Junior School

Racism Is Wrong

Racism is wrong and everyone knows it's true
So stop being racist come on, you know it too!
In the right time me and you know
You can stop being racist so stop it right now!
We are all the same; you shouldn't be a racist,
It hurts their feelings, no one likes being called racist names, it's wrong.

Amanda Bird (11)
East Park Junior School

Stop it

Stop cutting down trees
Lovely green healthy trees
You're killing animals' homes
Stop cutting them down.
You're killing beautiful animals
But you won't find any camels.
I know who your boss is Kevin
But you're sending oxygen to Heaven.
Stop cutting down trees
Lovely green healthy trees
You're killing bears, elephants, bats,
And even wild cats
So stop it!

Cameron Jones (10)
East Park Junior School

Don't Drop Litter

L ook after the world
I mprove the environment
T ogether we can help
T oday and tomorrow, we can save the world
E xtraordinary things can happen
R euse, recycle and reduce
   Don't drop litter, it could be dangerous.

Chloe Lewis (11)
East Park Junior School

Famine

Mothers live in fear
As they cry here, here.
Babies rub their swollen tummies
As they cry for their mummies.
Mothers discover that
Their children will suffer.
People get covered in lots of flies
Even in their little eyes.
People have no decent clothes to wear
It's all just wear and tear.

Amy Lewis (11)
East Park Junior School

Litter

Don't drop litter,
Put it in the bin.
Don't harm animals,
Keep the environment clean.
Don't bring rats in to our world
So once again, don't drop litter,
Litter is wrong.

Kayleigh Hill (11)
East Park Junior School

Extinction

E xtinction, extinction , stop extinction
X -ray fish have been poisoned
T rees lost, animals suffer
I nsect squashed by acid raindrops
N ature will never be at peace
C at families cry for mercy
T he monkey is moaning as the wind keeps blowing
I cebergs melting, water rising
O xygen has its dark side
N ow animals sleep in horror.

Ashleigh Pilsbury (11)
East Park Junior School

Litter

L is for litter being dropped on the floor
I is for individuals destroying our planet
T is for trapped animals struggling to escape
T is for trees chopped down and lost
E is for extinction, animals disappear
R is for rats with rabies running through our streets.

Sarah Louise Bagshaw (11)
East Park Junior School

Litter

The rats come out on Friday night for a nice delight
The sea dies as the Earth cries the people of the town sigh.
Litter sneaks its way into the sewer the rats become fewer and fewer
Litter in a race to make the world a horrible place.
Litter, litter, litter's bitter!

Kay Ann Allen (10)
East Park Junior School

Litter

Do not drop me because I'm litter
If you do I'll cover you in glitter.
Put me in the bin, that's where I belong,
If you do I'll sing a song.
Please clean me up,
But don't put me in a cup.
Looking after our world
Will help the environment build.

Charlie Crawford (11)
East Park Junior School

Poor Sam

Sam has a swollen tummy
He hasn't even got a mummy.
Too weak to walk upon thin legs
His friends so tired but have no beds.
Although homelessness is really rough
You have to be really tough.
His life is extremely hard
Guess what? He sleeps on card.

Emma White (11)
East Park Junior School

Healthy Eating

Healthy eating is such fun
Cook some veg, it's almost done.

Eat some fruit, that's not one
We're almost there, look they're gone.
You've followed well, you're fit and healthy
In fruit and veg, you'll be so wealthy.

Dionne Sherelle Abrahams (11)
East Park Junior School

The Rainforest

R aining, raining, raining,
A nimals getting wet
I nside their
N atural habitat
F urry animals dropping hair
O n the
R ainforest
E very day
S eeking
T he animals out.

Danny Homer (11)
East Park Junior School

Recycling Is Bitter

Ink, cans, bottles and card
Recycling things isn't hard.
Plastic, rubber and glass
We can be as green as grass.
Don't drop litter,
Instead be a recycling critter.
Don't drop disgusting litter
Pick it up and don't be bitter.
Put it in your pocket
Don't waste time and don't drop it.

Brandon Parker (11)
Fallings Park Primary School

Litter

Litter makes school un-cool
It sometimes kills animals
Litter doesn't ever fool
Bins are for litter
They help keep the streets clean
For some animals it's bitter
If you are in a car don't throw litter out your window
The window is to let breeze in
Next time you are in the car don't let litter get out
If you see some litter pick it up and put it in the bin
Then we can win!

Amy Newton (11)
Fallings Park Primary School

Poisonous Pollution

When we make a capacious fire
Gasses embark higher and higher.
But when the Earth shatters up in flames
I wonder who will be to blame.
Halt! Stop making such a fuss
Go and catch the local bus.
When you get to school, stop and think
Do I really need my car, school's not very far.
Where are you going, if it's not far
Then why don't you get out of your car!

Daniel Faulkner (11)
Fallings Park Primary School

Endangered

Squealing and crying
Animals dying
All over the face of the world
How can you just sit there
On your comfy chair
While these animals are being killed?

Polar bears and penguins
Living on the ice and snow
Even when it's melting away though
They are becoming extinct
And you are making their world shrink
In a couple of years they will be gone.

Birds and squirrels
Living in trees
When you cut them down
You are destroying the nest of bees
So stop cutting down
Those lovely breathing trees.

Jessie Ansell (11)
Fallings Park Primary School

Litter

L eaving litter
I s a crime let's get CSI.
T he person who dropped it, is a fool
T o people who dropped it is just fun
E verything you should just
R ecycle.

Ravan Chahal Singh (9)
Fallings Park Primary School

Litter

Don't drop litter put it in your pocket,
It harms animals so don't drop it.
Litter makes the ground look a mess
Pick it up and there'll be less.

Animals suffer every day
You will be the one who has to pay.
Animals get trapped in your baked beans tin
So put your litter in the rubbish bin.

This is a disgrace
It's all over the place
So come on, let's get green
To make our area clean.

Taylor Jefimik (11)
Fallings Park Primary School

The Recycling Rap

Don't be a fool
Try to be cool
Put a tin
In the recycling bin.
We won't make waste into paste
Banana peels and all the fruit
Skin and animal droppings
Make it into compost like Mary Poppins.
It's the little things that make a big difference.

Taneesha Lewis (9)
Fallings Park Primary School

Recycling

R ecycling is the best,
E ven better than all the rest,
C ans can go in the recycling bin,
Y es please recycle all the waste,
C ompost is made from some fruit peelings,
L eave the bin in a sunny dry spot,
I n the bin will be perfect compost,
N othing can beat recycling,
G et waste and put it in the bin!

Sonia Puri (9)
Fallings Park Primary School

Litter

Please don't drop litter; it's so repulsive and so bitter
It will make our school look disgusting and un-cool.
Animals die and people have to say bye bye.
Don't drop litter; it's so, so bitter
So put your bottles and tins in those useful bins.
Now recycle your paper and help your town become safer.
Don't drop it, put it in your handy pocket.

Courtney Haynes (10)
Fallings Park Primary School

I Hate War

War is terrible, war is bad
War makes lots of people sad.
I hate war, others do too,
It affects people like me and you.
War is fought with gun in hand,
Over a bit of silly land.
War is silly, I don't know why
You shouldn't bomb people in planes you fly.
Why should we fight it out?
It leaves people in a permanent pout.
I hate war, you should too,
So watch out if they try to bomb you!

Harry Chiam (10)
Four Oaks Primary School

Crossing Climate Change

Global warming is upon us
Lights left on, engines running
Out of a car and into a bus
Because if we don't changes are coming.
After your swim, get into the shower
Laying in the bath wastes a lot more power.
Wind power is better for our planet
And appalling weather will affect everyone on it.
Rain will be acid, ice caps will fall
My warning to you is if nothing changes, God help us all!

Georgia Davies Winkless (11)
Four Oaks Primary School

Make The World A Better Place

No matter what the colour of your skin
We are all the same people within.
We may be different on the outside
What matters is that you are nice inside.

It doesn't matter where you're from or how you speak
If you think it does, that makes you weak.
We have put up with racism for too long
Stand up and help, come on, be strong.

I feel sad but hope is still there
So don't be mean, please do be fair.
Help the nation to become stronger
Put up with racism for no longer.

Please read my poem with lots of care
After all, it was to help and to share.
How would you feel if people were racist to you?
If you'd be unhappy, they would be too!

Emma Hogg (11)
Four Oaks Primary School

What Do You Think?

We live in a world in which footballers are paid a lot
But we live in a world where people are poor.
We live in the world where film stars are paid millions
But we live in a world where people sleep on the street.
We live in a world of obesity
But we live in a world of hunger.
I think this is wrong!

Courtney Jones (11)
Four Oaks Primary School

It Isn't Meant To Be Like This

I look into the sky and what do I see
I see a world that was meant to be.
But how we are misusing it is extremely bad
And the thought of losing it makes me feel very sad.
Ruining this planet is such a big disgrace
Because we are damaging the environment and the human race.
Saving the planet is all of our concern
Here are the tips that we should learn.
Recycle, reduce, reuse
If we don't we have so much to lose.
I get cross when I look around
At all the litter lying on the ground.
If everyone did their part
Helping this planet, we would make a start.

Rebecca Cooper (11)
Four Oaks Primary School

Recycle

R ecycle your waste, be
E nergy efficient, reduce
C arbon emissions
Y ou can make a difference
C limate change, let's stop it
L ove the planet, our
E arth is valuable.

Benjamin Knowles (11)
Four Oaks Primary School

Recycling

Recycle, reduce, reuse
It's simple if you use these clues.
Put your glass in the recycling bins
Do the same with your plastics and tins.
Don't waste paper, recycle it, you know how,
Don't wait till tomorrow, start right now.
Reduce the rubbish you throw away
Not next year, moth or week but today!
Turn your heating down or even off
Keep warm with exercise or wearing more cloth.
It's important to do this for the sake of our planet
If it can't be recycled, reduced or reused, we should ban it.
Take action after hearing my plea.
The survival of our planet rests with you and me.

Beth Woodward (11)
Four Oaks Primary School

Animals And Extinction

If we don't look after our world all the animals will die.
So we need to think about the environment.
So get off your couch and do your bit for the animals.
Walk, cycle to work, stop polluting the air
Then our polar bears will have a place to live in.
Recycle paper, plastic, glass and metal
So I hope you do *your* bit!

George Brayford (11)
Four Oaks Primary School

Make Poverty History

What do you see on the news today?
People in poverty, torture and dismay
Their homes destroyed, lives shattered
But we still complain about our lives
Not caring for fellow humans.

No water, shelter and food
Their lives are in danger
What could we do to save them
What will be left tomorrow?

We must take action to save them
Even if it's a small amount
Every penny counts
So don't hesitate, help make poverty history
And you too will make a difference to other countries!

Safiyah Iqbal (11)
Hearsall Community Primary School

Climate Change

What happened to our summer's sun?
What happened to our rain?
Why are the seasons changing in many different ways?
Has summer fallen asleep?
Does winter have a cold?
Are they changing round to fight illness before they turn old?
Are we doing something wrong?
Do we need to change our actions?
Does God mean to punish us in many different ways?

Kiana Richardson (10)
Hearsall Community Primary School

Animals Near Extinction

Lots of animals are near extinction
What I'm telling you is not fiction
Think of the polar bears
They're needing more food and care
The tigers are killed for their fur
That definitely doesn't make them purr.
Fakes are killed just for fun
It gives everyone a bit of a stun.
These animals need as much help as they can get
Because they're not treated as well as your pet.

Phoebe May Emerson (11)
Hearsall Community Primary School

Recycling

R eproduce things
E very little thing makes a big difference
C lean up the world
Y ou can recycle old clothes
C ard can give a lot of energy if recycled
L ive a clean life
I f every boy and girl recycled it would make the world
  a happier place
N ature can also make a difference to there world
G ardens have compost to recycle.

Dineo Masiane (10)
Hearsall Community Primary School

Back Alley

He lay in the back alley waiting for the dark of the night
He dare not fall asleep because it might, he was right
Rain, rain, all through the night.

He trudges away in his soggy wet clothes
Where he's going nobody knows
He wanders aimlessly where no light shines.
This happens everywhere, but you don't care
How are we helping?

Connor Young (11)
Hearsall Community Primary School

Recycle Is A Good Thing

R eproduce to help the need
E verything you recycle will help the cause
C ollect as many things as you can
Y our choice can save the world
C are for the less fortunate people
L ittering is worse but if you recycle you can make
   the world responsible
E veryone in the world has tried to recycle, so it's your choice, recycle!

Zanele Mhlanga (11)
Hearsall Community Primary School

Recycle

Recycling is an easy job
How hard can it get?
Recycling is so simple
We shouldn't throw away
Recycling is our duty
Recycling is not far away
Next time we'll think
Why do we throw away?
We love recycling
We hate throwing away
There is no point in throwing away
Recycling is the best way.

Abdullah Khan (11)
Hearsall Community Primary School

Recycle

R euse products
E njoy recycling
C elebrate life
Y our choice
C lothes, recycle them
L ife is for living not suffering
E at fruit, any waste, recycle it.

Keisha Hibbert (11)
Hearsall Community Primary School

Littering Is Wrong

L ittering is wrong
I f you see a piece of litter pick it up
T ake care of your streets
T ake pride in where you live
E ven you can make a difference
R educe the amount of litter.

Ross Jordan Hatt (11)
Hearsall Community Primary School

It's Running Out Of Time, The World Might Die

Save the world, time's running out,
Don't be lazy quit going in the car
Or share the car.
Why leave the tap running?
Save the world, save the world,
Be happy with Earth,
Save the world.
Please help!

Jonathan Faulkner (8)
Lyndon Green Junior School

Save The World!

R ecycle! That's what you gotta do!
E veryone needs fresh air! So do you!
C ome on you can help us make the world a better place!
Y ou throw too much litter away. We need to stop it now!
C reate a happier world!
L ive a happier life in a cleaner world.
E veryone can help! Including you!

Amy Nicholas (8)
Lyndon Green Junior School

Litter Dumps

L itter is terribly bad,
I t changes our world to a horrible place.
T alk and make it better.
T ry to make it better and cleaner.
E veryone hates litter.
R eally try and help us make the world a better place.

Reece Wyatt (8)
Lyndon Green Junior School

Nature Dying

The air is polluted,
Time's running out,
Plants and bees are dying,
No water is a drought,
We are running out of water and energy,
There is too much traffic,
Just walk,
Don't go in the car,
Save the world!
Save the world!
Please I beg you,
Get up lazy bones,
Just get walking,
Please save the world!
Please save the world!
Please, please I beg you!
Save me!
Save my children!

Joshua Beer (8)
Lyndon Green Junior School

The Horrible World

This despicable, dirty disgrace
Makes this world a disgusting place.
We need to help the world,
We need to help the world.
It's being cruel to animals,
It's being cruel to others.
So recycle, reuse as well,
Do all that you can,
So shout, 'Reduce, reuse, recycle'.

Grace Tavner (7)
Lyndon Green Junior School

Help The World!

Time is running out,
Turn off electricity,
Share a car,
Use your legs,
Now it's time to stop,
We're going to be polluted,
Recycle paper,
Recycle bottles,
Have a 2 minute shower.
Help the world!
Save the world!
Hurry up,
Don't open windows when it's cold,
Don't use so much coal,
Time is running out.

Darcie Brady (7)
Lyndon Green Junior School

Save The World

Plants are dying
Don't waste water
Take two minute showers
Antarctic is melting
Hurry we might die
Pick up rubbish
Recycle stuff
It's almost gone
So are we
So hurry up!

Aiden Everett (8)
Lyndon Green Junior School

Save The World

Save the world,
Power is running low,
Cars are pumping smoke,
Go on a bike,
Use your legs to walk,
Turn your lights off,
Don't leave taps running,
Compost heap needs more,
Save the world,
Cold in the air,
Shorter time,
No one will be left,
We will be extinct.

Amy-Leigh Tuffield (8)
Lyndon Green Junior School

Time Is Running Out

Save the world,
Time is running out,
Share a car,
Use your bike,
Energy is running low,
Short showers,
Collect water,
Don't leave taps running,
Shut windows and your doors,
Recycle rubbish,
Plants are dying,
Animals are losing home,
Time is running out.

Rebecca Lily Sumner (7)
Lyndon Green Junior School

Please Help!

The Earth is polluted,
Turn off lights,
Turn off water,
Recycle rubbish,
Please help the world,
Use less coal,
Put washing on the line,
Turn off computers,
Shut windows,
Two minute showers,
Give to charity,
Use the sun to dry,
Time is running out,
Share cars,
Go on a bus,
Don't be lazy,
Please help!

Zack Yeomans (7)
Lyndon Green Junior School

Precious World

Turn lights off,
Always walk,
Never drive,
Help the world,
Stop pollution,
Turn taps off,
Help the world from pollution,
Time is running out,
The plants are dying,
Don't be lazy,
If plants die
We will die.

Ryan Thomas (8)
Lyndon Green Junior School

Save The World

Save the world,
Power is low,
Not much time left
To save the world,
So turn lights off,
Share a car,
Use public transport,
Trains and buses are empty,
Have shorter showers,
Don't leave taps running,
So now you know
How to save the world.

Emma Louise Hanson (7)
Lyndon Green Junior School

Help Save Our World

Please help us,
Share a car,
Walk,
Go on a bike,
Any will do,
Just try now!
Fuel is running out!
Animals are extinct,
Buy one bag,
Two minute showers,
Try and save the world please!

Maisy Dewell (8)
Lyndon Green Junior School

Please Help The World

The world is weak,
The smoke in the air,
We need some help,
There is no more water,
Please help, the world is dying,
See the world
Used to be just as beautiful.
The air is polluted,
Creatures are dying,
Look at the smoke,
You have to help the world,
Turn the taps off,
Have a short shower,
We don't want to be in a state,
Pull the plugs out,
Turn off the switches,
No more coal,
No more heat.

Jessica Jane Milner (7)
Lyndon Green Junior School

Time Is Running Out, Can You Hear Me?

Save the world,
Time is running out,
Turn the lights off,
Shut the windows, shut the doors,
Quick showers,
Don't throw away a lot,
Give to charity,
Share cars!

Time is running out,
Can you hear me?

Abigail Finnegan (8)
Lyndon Green Junior School

Please Help The World

Please save the world,
Power is down,
Water is running,
The air is polluted,
We are losing fresh air,
Animals extinct,
People are in the car,
Computer is on standby,
The shower is running,
Everyone is using power!
Cars are driving,
Please walk
Or go on bikes or share a car.
Please save the world!

Callum Rose (8)
Lyndon Green Junior School

Days Are Running Out

Save the world!
The days are running out,
You're wasting time,
No time to shout.

Recycle rubbish,
Turn taps off,
Save electricity,
Keep windows shut.

Save the world!
The days are running out,
You're wasting time,
No time to shout.

Poppy Goddard (8)
Lyndon Green Junior School

Recycle Now!

Help the world!
No time to shout,
You're wasting time,
Share a car,
Turn off your tap,
Our world is being polluted now.
You are wasting electricity.
Recycle, recycle now,
Time is running out,
So don't shout,
Time is running out,
So don't shout,
Recycle paper,
Recycle bottles,
Come on recycle now.
Soon the planet will be destroyed!
So come on recycle now!

Alisha Haria (8)
Lyndon Green Junior School

The Poor World

Save the world,
It's getting poor,
The animals are dying,
But don't like it,
So save the world,
So save the world.
Please save the world.
Put rubbish in the compost heap,
Buy small boxes of food.

Christopher Jackson (8)
Lyndon Green Junior School

Breaking Earth

Save the world,
The world is dying,
It is crying,
Help save the world,
There is more rubbish,
Look up!
The Earth's breaking,
The cheetah can't run,
Birds have stopped flying,
Flowers drooping,
So many dying,
Share a car,
Use electricity better,
Recycling is good,
Hurry, help!
The world is falling apart,
Reduce! Recycle! Reuse!

Tori Leah Southall (7)
Lyndon Green Junior School

Pollution

Plants are dying,
The birds might not be flying,
No water is a drought,
The leaves can't sprout,
We're running out of electricity,
That counts on everyone including me,
So save the world!
It causes thunder in the sky,
All the people are asking why.

Nialls Harry Neville Whyley (8)
Lyndon Green Junior School

Reduce, Recycle, Reuse

Help us save the world,
Save the petrol,
Share a car,
Use your bike,
The fresh air is running out,
The cars are busy polluting,
We're running out of time,
Reduce, reuse, recycle,
Recycling is the last thing on your mind,
Reuse scraps of paper,
Turn off your computer,
Please save the world,
The world's getting weaker!

James Burnham (8)
Lyndon Green Junior School

Pollution - Acrostic

P ollution
O n it goes, stop it
L ever it away
L ook at it do something
U niquely bad
T hink
I rritating
O paque and still
N o!

Amie Woodward (9)
Roman Way First School

Rainforest

R ain in the air
A nd trees everywhere
I t's like a house for animals
N o! Don't chop them down
F or animals safety don't chop them down
O h, they're great
R eappear all over the world
E verlasting everywhere
S top chopping them down
T urn it around and let them grow.

Siana Diane Beard (7)
Roman Way First School

Litter - Acrostic

L itter is horrible
I n the bin, make sure it goes
T rash is not good for animals
T errific it is not
E njoying litter is not a good thing
R ubbish, rubbish, rubbish.

Jade Hunt (8)
Roman Way First School

Where Have The Animals Gone?

Go to the wild, have a look around
How many creatures can be found?
The whales, turtles, chimps and fish
All getting killed for food in a dish.

Charlie William Harris (7)
Roman Way First School

Recycle

Recycle every day
Recycle your plastic
And that does mean recycle your elastic
When you've finished with a tin
Put it in the bin
And you will be happy!

Catie Williamson (9)
Roman Way First School

Recycle Letter Poem

P is for paper
P is for plastic
P is for pollution
That isn't fantastic.

Ciera Browne (7)
Roman Way First School

Panda - Haiku

I am black and white
Please save me from extinction
No bamboo for me!

Rachel Govada (8)
Roman Way First School

Recycle

Recycle, recycle,
As you pass those green bins
Don't forget to recycle your tins,
As you pass
Recycle your glass,
Recycle, recycle,
Recycle your plastic
It is so fantastic,
Just to recycle
Your fantastic plastic.

Zoe Louise Nicholls (9)
Roman Way First School

Recycle

R euse
E agerly needed to be done
C an be very useful
Y ou can make a big difference
C arry the future
L ove the Earth
E ncounter more energy.

Liam Holmes (8)
Roman Way First School

World - Cinquain

World
Cluttered, smashed
Spinning, caring, heating
We can make a difference
Safe.

Mollie Goode (9)
Roman Way First School

Help!

Sit there begging for mercy,
But all they get is curses,
People in Africa have worried lives.

Making posters and advertisements,
It just does not work . . .
Actually get out there and do something now,
Make a difference *now!*

Gemma May Alice Sealey (11)
St Francis CE Primary School, Bournville

Disease

A disease about to kill an innocent
Taking so many lives
An unjust, unfair way of death
Coming to ruin a soul
Baby, mother and child, all targets
A disease killed an innocent.

Dominic Glynn (11)
St Francis CE Primary School, Bournville

Littering

Littering is common from many people who don't care.
People litter everywhere and anywhere.
Littering is bad, people should not do it.
People who litter should have a little more care.

Joseph Smith (10)
St Francis CE Primary School, Bournville

Why?

W hy is war always around?
A re the people who fight there having fun?
R ipping and shredding is all that comes.

P lease help people live better,
E ven when war is around,
A haven is what the people need.
C ities are being raised to the ground.
E arth, will it ever have its peace?

H it the war famine with a blow.
E ver can you glow if you stop war.
L ive your lives in harmony.
P lease help people live calmly.

L ives will be better, if you help . . .
I n the end there's always death.
F eed the poor and hungry,
E nd the wars with life.

Joshua Palmer (11)
St Francis CE Primary School, Bournville

Think

I'm starving, I'm starving for some food,
I need to eat like anyone should,
I've had an empty plate from the start.
It's never been full I'm tellin' ya mate,
I want some chicken and I want some drink,
How could you live like this? . . . Just think,
Think when you tip your food in the bin, in my village that's a sin.
When we watch the white man just like a savage
We think of our children who all day go and ravage.
So just think . . .
So just think.

Daniel Bagby (11)
St Francis CE Primary School, Bournville

What We Don't See

People of Kenya laugh,
They watch their children play.
They care and love their beautiful gifts,
But there's something we don't see . . .

The children play football with rag-made balls,
We smile at them,
They wave back,
But there's something we can't see . . .

We hold their hands, they laugh with joy
And no sorrow shows.
They sing their songs, and clap and dance,
But there's something we don't see . . .

The poverty!
The hurt!
The terrible things that happen!
How can we just stand and watch
When there are people dying in the world?
That's what we don't see!

Naomi Powell (10)
St Francis CE Primary School, Bournville

Think Of Our Earth Dead

Come on let's fight for all the flowers.
Come on let's save the Earth from death.
Please help this cause for the environment,
If you don't there will be no animals left.
Please help this cause to save the environment
And save people from disease.
Think of our Earth with black covered sky,
Nothing to breathe and no living life.
Please Lord, help our beautiful Earth.
Please Lord, help our beautiful sky.

Harry Cullotty (11)
St Francis CE Primary School, Bournville

Give To People Who Are Poor!

Why are people treated badly?
They have done nothing,
That is so sad.
Everyone has the right to live,
All you have to do is try and give.

People are poor,
We need world peace, stop the war!
Why should people suffer from war?
All you have to do is open the door.

If you disobey what people have said
You should be helpful and give instead.

Tazmin Vandriwala (11)
St Francis CE Primary School, Bournville

Go And Help!

Taking trees is taking lives.
With people in Africa in poverty,
Little children sitting on Africa's streets,
Terrified and crying,
Begging for any scrap of food.

Global warming happening now, with people scared.
What will happen?
Instead of a frown they need to help!
So get up, stand up, go and help these people,
Now!

Zoë Harrison (11)
St Francis CE Primary School, Bournville

War And Peace

W ar is a black hole sucking you into death
A nd a chilling and murderous blow on life,
R eeking of rotting lives and death.

A re you agreeing with this madness,
N early joining in yourself?
D o not become emblazed in war.

P lease do not go mad!
E verything about peace
A nd not fighting in war
C an save lots of people,
E nflamed in gore.

Angus Smith (11)
St Francis CE Primary School, Bournville

Give To The World

Stop, listen, look and see, some people are in poverty,
Poverty is a disgrace, it's not fair,
Just because people don't live there.

Why are people treated so bad?
They have done nothing, that is just sad.
Homeless people never get their dreams,
Never really get given from a lot of people as it seems.

People are very poor.
We need world peace so stop the war.
All you have to do is give them a hand and open the door.

Emily Jean Bullivant (11)
St Francis CE Primary School, Bournville

Don't Let Animals Go To Waste!

Think of the animals that live in the sea,
Think about the animals in the world with you and me.

Think about the animals that live on the land,
Think of the animals that live in the sand.

What about the animals that live in the sky,
And about the animals that learned how to fly.

What about the animals that sit on your plate,
All the animals will be extinct at this rate.

Think of the tiger that learned how to run
And about the ostrich that sits under the sun.

What about the animals that live on the farm,
What about the animals that do you no harm.

Animals matter in this world of ours,
Respect for the animals is respect for the world.

Rebecca Guy (11)
St Francis CE Primary School, Bournville

Help!

No houses, nothing to eat,
Finding food for every day,
People getting rid of trees, it's where they live,
Don't get paid for all their hard work,
So . . .
Let's go eco green.

Michael Lennox (11)
St Francis CE Primary School, Bournville

Help The World!

Please, please help the world,
By not keeping fuels in the air,
That's simply keeping it fair.
Hey! Why aren't you listening?

Fine then, kill all the cats, kill all the dogs,
Delete all the 'Go green' blogs!
Kill all the insects!
Human existence: chuck it in the bin!

Make the skies black with fuel,
Make the gods curse at you,
Make sure all the trees are gone,
Make sure the world is dead!

Now would you like that to happen?
So leave the world in a beautiful state,
So please, please help the world.

Anaya Bolar (11)
St Francis CE Primary School, Bournville

Stop Littering!

The world is amazing, wonderful too,
But the public are ambushing the streets with litter.
While others are helping, the rest aren't caring.
So please help, please care it may change with your prayer.
Do you want to destroy the environment?

Nathan Rees (11)
St Francis CE Primary School, Bournville

Earth Is Condemned To Hang

When Man cuts rainforests
He gives himself enough rope to
Hang the planet to death.

Jamie Tennant (11)
St Francis CE Primary School, Bournville

Africa Rap

We all need money and we're not being funny.
I've got a mummy but I very rarely see her 'cause she's making fur.

I'm working on a farm, it's very quiet and calm.
I don't like it at all.

I miss my son and daughter,
But I'm looking for fresh water,
If I don't get water, it will almost be a slaughter.

I really need the money and I'm not being funny,
I really love my mummy.

When I see a vine
I want to make a line
So I can die,
That's how sad I am.

Kallum O'Toole (11)
St Francis CE Primary School, Bournville

The Solution For Pollution

We need a solution
To stop the pollution
Walk to school
And don't be a fool
Turn off the tap
Or the lake will be off the map
Don't be mean
And go green!

Charlotte Lowe (8)
St Peter's Catholic First School, Bromsgrove

Helping The World

I have a solution for pollution,
We must walk to school and if we try . . .
We can help the sky!

We must use less electricity to help the world compete,
Otherwise our world would be in heat.

Animals, animals they are disappearing fast,
But if we work together we can make them last and last.

Recycle, recycle is something we must do,
We must help save our planet for me and for you.

With just a little thought we could all make a big difference,
By caring and sharing, and all using our common sense.

Briony Read (8)
St Peter's Catholic First School, Bromsgrove

Go Green Not Mean!

Stop being mean and start going green.
We need a solution to stop this pollution.
The pollution is causing diseases.
Put your rubbish in the bin
If you don't it is a sin.

Niamh Caffrey (9)
St Peter's Catholic First School, Bromsgrove

Recycling Is Bitter!

If you are bad and you litter
You will make the world bitter,
Rainforests will be destroyed
And children won't get any toys.
Recycling is the thing you should do,
If you don't want the world to smell like poo!
If you are in a war please, please, please,
Stay out of it and then you won't get a disease!
Animals and extinction are very important,
Being homeless and pollution is as well,
Poverty, climate change and racism come with it all,
'Pick that off the floor or I might tell!'

Chloe-Ann Rooney (9)
St Peter's Catholic First School, Bromsgrove

The Colour Green Is Not So Mean

Our planet is in trouble
So we must change on the double,
The animals are dying
Because litter keeps on flying,
We must recycle paper,
We can't leave it any later,
It is really cool to walk to school
So the colour green is not so mean!

Joseph Smith (8)
St Peter's Catholic First School, Bromsgrove

Do You Recycle?

Do you recycle? Yes I do.
Do you recycle? Yes you too,
Do you recycle plastic or elastic?
Just like the four they're fantastic!
I have a home where I recycle more,
Just like the Fantastic Four.
Do you recycle metal like a kettle?
Do you have wealth on your shelf?
Just like leaves on trees.

Holly Robinson (8)
St Peter's Catholic First School, Bromsgrove

Helping Hands

Please help the homeless and dogs that are boneless,
Help people with a disease,
You might not find any ease,
Pick up litter and things that are bitter
And give some more to the poor!
These are the things that make me happy,
Flowers and trees, butterflies and bees,
If you don't look after things there will be none left of these!

Katie Burke (8)
St Peter's Catholic First School, Bromsgrove

A Better World

Open the door to a new world,
Put your litter in the bin.
If you don't want the world to die out
You should start recycling.
So we say; buy less, recycle more,
Buy a bag for life they're a very cheap price.
Some day you people will see
If you use recyclable bags
And reduce the amount of rubbish,
Don't start polluting
Or spreading a disease
And not starting a war
The world will be a better friend for all.

Rebecca Macpherson (9)
St Peter's Catholic First School, Bromsgrove

Taking Action - Haiku

Pollution kills birds,
Poverty is all over,
We have to act now!

Eden Peppercorn (9)
St Peter's Catholic First School, Bromsgrove

Our World

Everyone in the world stop and think,
Because our planet is going down the sink.
We are wasting resources,
Left, right and centre.
Without drastic change
There will be no future.
Litter is bad we must make less,
Recycling is the way to avoid this mess.
Destroying our planet will lead to extinction,
We can all do our bit to reduce this pollution.
Animals in the rainforests are going one by one,
Because people can't resist the taste so they're shot down by
                                                                      the gun.

Rhiannon Edwards (8)
St Peter's Catholic First School, Bromsgrove

Worst War

Guns are firing,
People are dying.

We're wondering whether
We should leave our city,
To reach another town.

They run all alone
Till they get home.

Where they can have a happy life
Without fear of a gun and knife.

Hanad Arwo (10)
Woodhouse Primary School

Birds

Birds are dying every day,
Because they are human prey.

Hunters have a secret lair,
Shooting birds is just not fair.

Sitting on a chair every day,
Looking for their feathery prey.

Female birds try to find a male,
But they inevitably fail.

Walking in the forest every night,
I have no fear because birds don't bite.

Can't you leave the birds alone,
And let the chicks become fully grown.

Muhammad Zeeshan Sartaj (9)
Woodhouse Primary School

War And Sadness

You see demolishing towns,
Misery and frowns.

Stop all this madness,
Stop all this sadness.

Respect each other,
And help one another.

You go on a train,
Before you enter a place of pain
Dragging yourself through the rain.

So remember to respect the Earth
For all your worth.

Bradley Walton (10)
Woodhouse Primary School

Litter

Once there was a boy
Who dropped some litter
Because it was bitter.
The very next day,
A person came to say,
'I saw you drop some litter yesterday.'
'So what?' said the boy.
'So what you're saying,
Soon you'll be paying.'
'Why?' asked the boy.
'If you want to keep the environment clean,
You mustn't be so mean,
So be green!
So I suggest you listen to what I say,
Or otherwise you'll have to pay!'

Gurjeevan Chal (10)
Woodhouse Primary School

Save The Animals

Save all the animals,
Brown, white and blue,
'Cause you wouldn't like it
If they hunted down you.
If we keep destroying trees,
What'll be our solution,
If we cause a lack of oxygen
And also air pollution?
If we keep killing birds
And cut down their nest,
The little baby birds
Won't be able to rest.
What makes us different
To all the other mammals,
And we are the clever ones,
So we should save the animals.

Jay Copper (10)
Woodhouse Primary School

The Big Green Thing

The world would be a better place,
If you didn't have the litter all over the place,
With rainforests being cut down for a piece of paper,
You could just pick it up and put it in the recycler.

With animals all coming to extinction,
All you have to do is lay off the acceleration,
And when the world is dying of pollution,
All we're doing is watching television,
And we don't do a single thing,
When we could be doing something like recycling.

If you haven't listened to what I've said,
Suffer the consequences and everything will be dead!
If it sounds like I'm not telling the truth,
All the scientists in the world have the proof.

William Howes (11)
Woodhouse Primary School

Litter

When Messy Michael unwraps a sweet,
He throws the paper on the street,
He throws sticks and tins and banana skins,
And people can always say Messy Michael has been here today.

But if you see his brother Tidy Tim,
Nobody can throw litter beside him,
Because he likes the pavement nice and clean,
So no sticks are not to be seen,
And that's why he is called Tidy Tim.

Lily-May Miller (9)
Woodhouse Primary School

Rainforests

Water trickling down from leaves to the ground,
When people come there is not a sound,
Not a movement no, nowhere,
Why should we do this? It is not fair.

Can we not share the world with the animals
With the monkeys, the lizards and parrots?
You forget we are animals too.

Chopping wood,
Bringing blood,
It's terrible I know but it is what you are doing,
Stop this now!

Elizabeth Jane Thorpe (9)
Woodhouse Primary School

Recycling Your Way

R ecycling can help save the planet.
E ndangered species.
C ollection days for recycling.
Y ou can make a difference.
C an you save the animals from extinction?
L ocal recycling places are now open.
I think our planet needs more love and care.
N o more throwing away things that can be used again.
G o and recycle now before it's too late.

Irish Winkelmann (8)
Woodhouse Primary School

Save The Planet

In the busy street
You are stamping your feet,
While cars come past
Sending off carbon emissions.

The North Pole is melting,
Polar bears are sweltering,
Just do your part
To save the planet.

You can walk not drive,
Along with another five,
You can turn your light off
When you leave a room.

If we all work together,
You might see another feather
Drifting from the sky,
We can save the planet.

Nathan White (10)
Woodhouse Primary School

Cruelty To Animals

Cruelty to animals,
Big or small,
People go out to abuse them.
What happens next?
They take them out the back,
And the animals try to hack
The door locks,
While the clock tick-tocks,
The animal is starved to death,
They are not fed,
While the owner is in bed.

Mathew Riddle (9)
Woodhouse Primary School

Save The World

Save the place
The human race
The whole land
The place we stand
The animal kingdom
Really we should save 'em
Stealing in every shop
Please, please make it stop
The sun's coming closer
Don't just lie on your sofa
The place is covered with pollution
Please, we need a solution!

Létitia Treacy (9)
Woodhouse Primary School

Stop War Now

Guns are firing,
Innocent people are dying,
Now let's stop this horrible game . . . *now!*
Guns are loading,
Grenades are throwing,
People are getting blown up now.
Let's stop this sadness in the world
And get on together . . .
Now!

Luke Houghton (9)
Woodhouse Primary School

Pollution

P lease stop air pollution.
O h no the cars are steaming everywhere!
L ots of animals lose their worlds.
L et's help by stopping fumes.
U ndo all these horrid things please, please.
T ell your friends and family to help too.
I t's terrible, you'll lose your world.
O h, just *stop* all the fumes, *help* the world.
N ow get up and help our world!

You can make a difference!

Sophie Burrows (9)
Woodhouse Primary School

Recycle

R ecycle in the right bins.
E very time always recycle glass and bottles.
C areful you might hurt yourself on the glass.
Y ou never throw the recycling stuff on the floor.
C ans, bottles, glass should all be recycled.
L earn to love your environment.
E verywhere glasses and bottles should be recycled.

Jasmin Tantoco (7)
Woodhouse Primary School

Litter

L itterbugs are very dirty.
I n the streets there is lots of litter.
T issues are thrown on the floor.
T he world is very messy!
E veryone make the world clean!
R ecycle all your rubbish!

Holung Lee (8)
Woodhouse Primary School

Litter

L itter, litter on the floor, don't drop litter on the floor.
I f there is a paper on the floor put it in the bin.
T here is a bin around put the rubbish in the bin.
T hrowing litter on the floor that is being nasty.
E veryone that throws litter on the floor makes the street untidy.
R emember you should not throw litter on the floor because
that is being lazy.

Pariese Paul (7)
Woodhouse Primary School

Litter

L itter is a bad habit.
I t is naughty to throw rubbish on the floor.
T he litter takes years to fade away into the earth.
T he rubbish can harm wildlife.
E arth should be respected by everyone.
R ubbish should always be in the bins.

Casey Miller (8)
Woodhouse Primary School

War Is Bitter

War is bitter, it's not a better way!
Pollution is spread and animals run away.
Countries fall apart while people travel afar.
War ends, people come home but their families are lost.

Ákos Szücs (10)
Woodhouse Primary School

What's Happened To The Animals?

What's happened to the animals?
Will they become extinct?
Where have all the elephants gone?
They've been killed for their tusks.
Hunters must not kill. They have to stop.
What's happened to the animals?
Will they be extinct?
Where have all the zebras gone?
They've been killed for the fur.
Hunters must not kill. They have to stop.

Hadis Mohamadi (8)
Woodhouse Primary School

Polar Bears

Polar bears, polar bears hunt for a meal,
Polar bears, polar bears hunt for a seal.

Polar bears, polar bears creep upon the ice,
Polar bears, polar bears as quiet as mice.

The ice flows down into the sea gentle,
For we are driving the Earth mental.

We have caused this pollution,
But nobody has come up with a solution.

Charlotte Smith (9)
Woodhouse Primary School

Recycling

There is this little thing called recycling,
Which to some people is menacing,
It is very important so please do it,
Every day bit by bit!

Plastic, paper, glass and cans,
If you're doing it, carry on man!
Do it, do it, it's very good,
Please help save the world, change your mood!

If you carry on like this,
It'll be very bad,
You'll have fun with recycling,
It will save the world from going mad!

Meghana Vaidya (9)
Woodhouse Primary School

Litter

Litter, litter everywhere,
Litter, litter under the chair.
Litter, litter in your hair,
Oh yeah there is litter over there.

Litter, litter everywhere,
In the street and on the beach,
And in the pool it is not cool.
Pick it up quick
Before our planet gets sick.

Sara Elsharif (9)
Woodhouse Primary School

Trees

Trees, beautiful trees
Blowing in the wind
Swaying green leaves
Tough, textured bark
Branches stretched out like arms
Calling in the birds to nest.

Chop, chop the trees fall down
The birds fly away
Paper is made.

Recycle litter to save the trees
To save nature's homes
To make the world a better place.

Courtney Bonehill (8)
Woodhouse Primary School

Extinction!

Where have all the crocodiles gone?
They've been killed for boots, bags and belts.
Where have all the polar bears gone?
All the ice has melted.
Where have all the lions gone?
They've been killed for their fur.

Cameron Hadley (9)
Woodhouse Primary School

Litter

Litter, litter everywhere
In the playground, street and parks,
People throw their rubbish in the dark.
Please ask parents and friends,
So don't throw rubbish on the floor,
Throw it in the bin!

Shannon Byrne (9)
Woodhouse Primary School

Litter

Litter, litter everywhere!
We must help keep the country tidy,
So put your litter in the bin.
Recycle when you can!
Poor animals get hurt when we do not think.
They eat our litter and become weak,
Some may live, some may die.
Come on please,
Think!

Christian Lewis Bell (8)
Woodhouse Primary School

Litter

Don't drop rubbish on the floor,
It's a bad habit that's for sure.
Put your litter in the bins,
Packets, paper, bottles and tins.
Now the world is a cleaner place
For all the human race.

Mia Shannon (8)
Woodhouse Primary School

Litter

Litter, litter everywhere,
Makes you think, stop and stare,
Put it in the recycling bin,
If you don't it will be a sin.

Hema Chumber (7)
Woodhouse Primary School

Rainforest

The size of the rainforest is decreasing every second.
The rain is dropping on the leaves and it helps growing the trees.
The rainforest smells like tropical fruit swaying down
From the sweet green leaves of the tree.
The trees need the rain
And we need the trees to remain.
They help provide oxygen, that is why we need them.

Amardeep Chal (8)
Woodhouse Primary School

The Rainforest

The water falls, as the clear water streams,
With the heavy swish, swish of the waterfall stream.
The damp, humid smells of mist air.
Bright greens, dark greens, tree bark browns,
Those are the colours of the rainforest ground.
The rainforest.

Anisah Shabir (8)
Woodhouse Primary School

Litter

Litter, litter is falling down everywhere,
But the thing is no one cares.
So if the word recycle comes to them the litter, litter everywhere
                                                    will vanish.
So let's recycle and make a big difference.
Remember it's the little things which make a big difference!

Prashant Ramnatsing (8)
Woodhouse Primary School

Litter!

Lots of litter left on the streets.
In parks and towns, not in the bins.
The litter is a terrible mess,
Then it makes our world into a nasty place.
Everywhere rubbish is on the ground,
Remember put your litter in the bins not on the roads or streets.

Tahmid Kalam (8)
Woodhouse Primary School

Extinct Animals

Dodos and dinosaurs are all extinct,
We should look after elephants or there won't be any left,
The hunters are fighting
And the poachers are killing for money to make them rich,
It's very sad.

Ellie Louise Shannon (8)
Woodhouse Primary School

Police Say Stop!

Please don't throw
Your junk around.
All the police
Say it's not allowed.

Reece Taylor (7)
Woodhouse Primary School

Pollution

Pollution hangs around us everywhere.
Air pollution is smoke from factories and fumes from cars.
Pollution hangs around us everywhere.
Land pollution is litter causing bad smells
And it attracts rats . . . oh no.
Pollution hangs around us everywhere.
Water pollutions causes chemicals that farmers use on their crops,
It kills all the fish and animals
So please stop *pollution!*
Don't throw your litter away somewhere on the floor
Put it in the bin.

Holly Edwards (9)
Woodlands Primary School

Litter Bugs

Stop littering please! You're causing pollution.
The landfills are looking untidy and smelly,
They attract rats and nasty bugs and we don't want that do we?
In rivers and ponds fishes are getting killed
And that's not nice for them.
We don't want our world to be smelly and not looking nice.
So when you have rubbish throw it away
Or recycle it if it can be recycled.

Charlotte Maija Johnson-Howe (9)
Woodlands Primary School

Litter

Litter is being thrown everywhere,
But people do not care,
On the floor, not in the bin,
Don't let us down because we can win.

Cardboard, paper, tin and glass,
When we put it together it will be a mess.
Litter, litter everywhere,
I'm going to pull out my hair.
I am so, so sad but really mad.
Please do not leave rubbish on the floor . . .
Pick it up.

Emma Campbell (9)
Woodlands Primary School

Litter's Getting Worse!

Litter piling up in the gutter,
Litter polluting the sea,
Litter crowding the main streets,
Oh please, please, please help me
To help clear up all the litter,
And stop people getting ill,
In other countries it may be worse,
So come on binmen you know the drill!

Amy Hampshire (11)
Woodlands Primary School

Litter

Stop throwing rubbish on the floor,
You are attracting all flies and rats,
You're making this world smell of rubbish,
Errh we won't like that.
Why is everybody throwing rubbish?
There are bins, so put your rubbish in there,
Do not put your wrappers on the floor,
Stop the people leaving dog mess everywhere.
I think it is time to tidy up,
Nobody wants a dirty world to live in.

Lucy Stirling (8)
Woodlands Primary School

The Animal Poem

Animals are dying because of us,
They are getting trapped in cans,
Swallowing litter so they die,
They are swallowing stuff so they get cut,
So please help the animals all the time.
Help animals that are becoming extinct all the time,
Polar bears, snakes, lions and seals
And loads more that are extinct.
So please help animals that are in danger,
So please help animals that are dying,
Please help animals.

Megan Hampshire (9)
Woodlands Primary School

Litter

Litter is super smelly, you would not like to meet some,
If you do you'd better get a peg and put it on your nose.
It attracts all the rats and cats and flies
So you'd better watch out it don't look very nice,
It would never win the prettiest competition.
Don't throw it in ponds, rivers, lakes and streams,
Just put it in the bin.
It's killing everything so put it in a bin, a recycling bin
Or a bag or the dump if you can stand the smell.

Hannah Bullows (8)
Woodlands Primary School

The Siberian Tiger

This creature is the largest living cat in the wild,
With grace and beauty to match,
Lying in the hot jungle sun,
These animals weigh a tonne,
They are true carnivores,
However these amazing creatures are becoming a rare sight
                                                            in the wild.

Laura Carless (11)
Woodlands Primary School

Don't Drop Your Litter

If you're feeling bitter,
Please don't drop your litter,
Even on a rainy day!

If you're feeling down,
Don't give a frown,
Clean up your litter today!

So if you see some litter,
Don't just bicker,
Green is on the way!

There are plastic bags,
Paper cups,
Even mouldy food,
McDonald's bags,
Dirty rags,
What a dreadful attitude!

Emily Spittle (10)
Woodlands Primary School

Fish Kennings

Bubble blower,
Hook victim,
Water lover,
Corn eater,
Fisherman's dream,
Rod bender,
Slimy character,
Scale keeper,
Speed demon,
Top feeder,
Bottom lying.

Alan Melling (11)
Woodlands Primary School

The Greener World

The world is round,
It rolls on the ground.
Make it greener,
Make it see ya.

Make the world bright,
Make it like a light.
Don't drop litter,
Don't be bitter,
Put it in the bin
So we win.

Put your paper
In the recycle bin,
Save our trees,
Also our bees,
Our animals are dying,
So get flying with your recycling
And save our trees.

Victoria Bird (9)
Woodlands Primary School

Recycle It!

The trees are blue because of us!
Everybody everywhere hear me now,
Do you want forests and do you want to breathe?
Recycle your things and stop global warming,
Help us and get what we want.
Recycle to help the planet!

Joshua Pullinger (9)
Woodlands Primary School

Seagulls Are Dying

Seagulls are already rare
So please be careful because they are dying from this,
So stop it quick.
Stop people if you can.
Try your best please, do it now or they will die immediately.
Please try your best, I'm begging you pretty please.
Try your best, really do or go away for good,
I really hope you do.

Joseph Turton (8)
Woodlands Primary School

Recycle

Recycle your tins in your little green bins to reduce.
Reuse and recycle to build cars, planes and different vehicles,
So please try to keep our world tidy.
It's not best for us, it's best for you,
If you don't you might have some rats and cats in your home,
So put your cans, paper and glass bottles in green bins or boxes.

Jaye Roberts (8)
Woodlands Primary School

Litter

Littering is bad so please make it stop,
It attracts filthy animals.
Don't drop it, pick it up!
And we could win the cleanest cup.
It's a bad habit, so will you stop it?
It's trapping small animals, so please don't drop it,
Put it in the bin!

Sam Bradley (9)
Woodlands Primary School

Arctic Foxes

Some of us are getting upset
Because some of the people are killing Arctic foxes.
Please, please stop, we like these foxes.
Why do you do it?
It makes us cry.
Arctic foxes mean a lot, they're becoming something their not.
These foxes are becoming extinct.
Help them by stopping these killers.

Megan Annie Clayton (9)
Woodlands Primary School

Litter, Litter, Litter!

Litter makes the world look a mess,
People unlikely to put rubbish in the bin.
Lakes, ponds and rivers are getting packed with junk,
It's killing wildlife more each day.
We all need to help, to do something
About the litter, the junk and the rubbish.

Lucy Emma Ball (9)
Woodlands Primary School

Litter

Litter is being thrown on the floor,
When animals come along they are getting hurt in it.
Animals are dying so we have to take action,
If we don't do anything now the animals are all going to die.
Please, if you see any litter on the floor pick it up
And put it in the bin!

Chloe Freeman-Chick (9)
Woodlands Primary School

Litter

Litter is super smelly, it will attract all the rats.
All the flies will be on it but you wouldn't like it at all.
Litter looks very untidy because it is everywhere.
It is in ponds, rivers and streams,
Also bubblegum on the floor
And bonfires all over the floor as well.
It is not very good that there is all kinds of things on the floor.
Litter is everywhere in the world.

Demi-Leigh Hems (8)
Woodlands Primary School

Litter

Litter makes the world look a mess,
Lots of litter can be dangerous,
It can cause an accident,
It will attract all the rats,
Litter gets thrown into ponds and animals will not survive,
Litter is pollution,
Litter is everywhere.

Brooke Holland (7)
Woodlands Primary School

Litter

Litter makes the world look untidy,
People don't care about animals and throw junk in the lake.
Litter and rubbish floods the lake,
It kills wildlife all day long.
It attracts rats, cats and flies.
We all need to do something to help the environment.

Sophie Hampshire (8)
Woodlands Primary School

Recycle

R ecycle,
E verywhere there is rubbish, rubbish, rubbish,
C ans can be recycled lots and lots,
Y ou can recycle litter too.
C ollections can stop waste,
L itter is rubbish, rubbish, rubbish,
E rase the mistakes we have made and make it a better place.

Jessica Lockley (9)
Woodlands Primary School

Litter

Why should we put up with all of your stinky litter?
I object to put up with it.
It's awful.
One day it will get so suffocating!
It's mean, it causes diseases.
Why are we so mean at times?
So let's get rid of the stink and reduce, reuse, recycle.

Chloe Babiy (9)
Woodlands Primary School

Litteration!

L itter needs to get off our road
I think the world is going to explode
T he world wants to be your chum
T he green machine is the best hum
E ven one of your family members couldn't be kind
R ags and clothes will be at the back of our mind!

Millie Slater (10)
Woodlands Primary School

You!

You! Your face is like a fluffy pug dog.
You! Your eyes are like big black marbles.
You! Your nose is like a raisin.
You! Your ears are like two black oranges.
You! Your hands are like soft, small, black pillows.
You! Your arms are like floppy teddy bears.
You! Your legs are like furry fat sticks.
You! Your feet are like spiky thorn needles.
You! Your stomach is like a big boulder.
You! Your bottom is like a pig's bottom.
You! Your tail is like a bunny's tail.

Please help pandas from extinction!
You will never know if this description is true!

Leia Walker (8)
Woodlands Primary School

Where Are All The Animals?

Where are all the animals?
Animals are dying, all because of us.
Trapped in cans, trapped in boxes,
It's really all our fault.
But animals can be saved,
If we try harder.
Maybe they will come back,
And make our world better.

Abigail Whistance (7)
Woodlands Primary School

Animals

Animals are in the streets,
They're smelly everywhere.
Let's all find them a good home,
Maybe over there.
Somewhere there is a home,
Not too smelly, not too fresh.
Let's all give them a fab home
That does not cause them a death.
So let's all do something new,
So they don't make litter in the street.
So let's all find them a home,
For these lovable animals we meet.

Rachael Burgess (10)
Woodlands Primary School

Litter

Litter is super smelly,
It will attract all the rats and flies
And it will look untidy.
It is everywhere,
It is in ponds and rivers all day long
With bubblegum on the floor,
It is not a pretty sight.
So please pick it up, it is everywhere.

Emily Watton (8)
Woodlands Primary School

Help Us Animals

We are the animals of the world
And we need your help because we are becoming extinct.
I am a polar bear and I am nearly extinct
Because my homeland is melting very fast
Even though we can last just a little bit longer,
We need your help.
I am a leopard and I am becoming extinct
Because my skin is being hunted to make nice coats,
But it is not nice for us.
Please help us!
I am a human and I am not extinct
But I am going to help all the animals that are becoming extinct.

Sophie Green (8)
Woodlands Primary School

Litter

Please stop throwing litter into ponds,
It's killing animals
And stop throwing it on the floor
It is attracting unpleasant rats,
It looks untidy and smells horrible.
Don't throw it in rivers,
It's making animals extinct
Like certain types of fish in rivers.

Nathan Reeves (8)
Woodlands Primary School

Recycle

R ecycle things to make the world green,
　　the world will be more seen.
E verlasting paper
　　is way more safer.
C ollect rubbish in littered places,
　　make people have a smile on their faces.
Y ou can play a part in this,
　　all you have to do is wish.
C an you do it? Yes you can,
　　cutting down trees is bad.
L ook around, what do you see?
　　Fresh ground for you and me.
E nough room for everyone.

Kelsey Bentley (10)
Woodlands Primary School

Why We Should Recycle

Recycling is good for you,
It's even good for the animals too!
Recycling isn't that bad that it will make you die
But please, please really try,
Put your crisp packets in the bin
And promise me you won't fall in!
Make sure you're no litterbug,
Instead of throwing it away keep it and give it a hug!

Sophie Ann Thorpe Gogerty (9)
Woodlands Primary School

Save The Environment

Litter in the hedges, rubbish in the street,
Bubblegum on the pavements, it's not very sweet.
It's hurting the wildlife, you're throwing them out of their homes,
Birds from a nest, bats from a loft, bunnies from a burrow.
Coming down with an infection, coming down with a disease,
So do help us, so do help us please.
War is arriving, people are fighting,
Friends are dying, fires are lighting.
Who is making a mess? Who is littering the world?
It's anonymous, it's a mystery, it's absurd.
Save the environment, save the planet,
Then there's a better world to let.

Ellie Valerie Dobell (10)
Woodlands Primary School

Polar Bears

Polar bears, polar bears
Are so big!

Polar bears, polar bears
Need more clean air.

To help our lovely polar bears to survive
Be a good friend and turn your plugs off!

All the ships with your nets
Only catch the fish you need.

Jordan Saunders
Woodlands Primary School

Rubbish

I will not litter because I am mad.
I will not litter because I am mad.

I will dream of a world that is clean.
I will dream of a world that is green.

I will not litter because I am sad.
I will not litter because I am glad.

I will dream that the sky is clear.
I will dream that toxic fumes I no longer need to fear.

Charlotte Spink (10)
Woodlands Primary School

Climate Change

The melting ice caps
Are becoming a problem.
It's getting hotter,
It is serious!
We need to recycle more,
To get a future
In the world we're in,
Otherwise it will be bad
For eternity!

Samuel Parkes (10)
Woodlands Primary School

Save Our Planet

Save our planet,
Make it happen.
Recycle paper, plant more trees,
Pick up litter, get rid of disease.
Save our animals,
They're getting extinct.
I dream we would stop . . .
Litter, pollution, homelessness, disease,
War, cutting down trees
And lots, lots more.
Save our planet,
Make it *happen!*

Shân Jones (10)
Woodlands Primary School

Being Homeless

Everyone listen to me,
I've got a story about a lady called Lea,
She has no home,
No bed to sleep in,
She lives on the street
With very cold feet,
She has no friends,
No family to love,
Everyone listen to me,
I've got a story about a lady called Lea.

Emma Garley (10)
Woodlands Primary School

Save Our World

Make our world greener
By being cleaner.
Don't be a weed,
Do a deed.
Don't drop litter,
Don't let it flitter
Around the streets.
Animals are dying out,
Scream and shout.
Save the people from disease,
Stop exhaust fumes
So people no longer sneeze and wheeze.

Hollie Jones (9)
Woodlands Primary School

Animals And Extinction

Orang-utans,
Pandas,
Very, very rare,
Frogs and dogs
There are so many to spare.
Help the animals,
Help them survive!
Don't shoot and kill,
Leave them be.
Animals deserve to live,
Just like you and me.

William Davis (10)
Woodlands Primary School

Litter!

Litter, litter should not be done,
Do you think the Earth thinks its fun?
Come on, pick it up,
Don't just stand around,
Don't leave litter on the ground!

Littering should not be done,
If you pick it up you won't feel glum!

Litter, litter
It's everywhere.
Pick it up before it's done,
Don't leave litter on the ground!

Holly Crook (10)
Woodlands Primary School

War

War, war,
Why so much war?
Fighting,
Crying,
But no smiling,
People worried,
People scared,
Why won't it ever end?

Patrick Patton (9)
Woodlands Primary School

The War Poem

War, war, there's too much war,
Too many people are dying,
People like you and me
And other families.
So panic! Panic! There's too much war!
War, war, there's too much war,
We must do something more,
So stop the war, there's too much war,
Or soon we'll all die.
So please stop, oh please, please stop
These terrible fights called war.

Callum Lewis Street (10)
Woodlands Primary School

Save Our Planet

Litter, litter it's just bitter,
It's everywhere I go.
Mess, mess it's not the best,
Think about poor birds in a nest.
War, war it's everywhere,
Why can't we just take care.
Homeless, homeless it's just a mess,
Come on people and just confess.
Reuse, reuse you can't get confused
And if you do, we won't lose.

Paris Mai Lawrence (10)
Woodlands Primary School

Untitled

War, war everywhere,
Why do they do it?
Do they like it?
I don't think so!
It's not right.

Bullets flying!
Bombs exploding!
People dying!

War, war everywhere,
Why do they do it?

Adam Walters (10)
Woodlands Primary School

Litter

When you see litter, it looks such a mess,
Litter in the gutter,
It is a pest.

Litter on the ground,
Rubbish on the road,
Chewing gum just left around,
We could fill a lorry load.

Rebecca Mills (10)
Woodlands Primary School

Litter Poem!

Litter, litter, pick up your litter,
Do you think the Earth likes the litter?
Come on, pick it up, don't just stand around,
No more games, no more fun,
Even the sun doesn't like it to be done!
This is sad, not very glad,
Don't leave litter on the ground.

Leah Wilkinson (10)
Woodlands Primary School

Pollution

Cars, cars everywhere,
Putting pollution in the air,
Factories working now and then,
Hiring more and more men,
People coughing to get clean air,
Everyone knows it isn't fair,
Everyone's stressing and losing their hair,
Everyone knows this isn't fair.

Bethany Haddon (10)
Woodlands Primary School

Litter

Don't leave rubbish on the floor
Otherwise there will be a war.
Put your rubbish in a bin
Otherwise it will be a sin.
Littering should not be done,
Animals don't think it's fun.
Don't leave litter on the ground,
Come on, pick it up don't just stand around.

Sophie Richards (10)
Woodlands Primary School

Litter

L ittering should not be done
I see it all day long
T ime to stop and change your ways
T oday's the day to be part of the game
E at your lunch and put it in the bin
R ubbish, rubbish, rubbish.

Abbie Chester (10)
Woodlands Primary School

Forests

We need to save the forests with all the bugs and rats
And the deep dark caves full of low flying bats.
There are lots of monkeys, birds and bees,
The plants grow so fast - at an enormous rate,
We need to stop destroying the forest before it is too late,
Stop now before we make all the rainforests a dreadful state.

Max Rushton (10)
Woodlands Primary School

War!

War,
We should have no more war,
People fall,
People die,
So no more war,
Please, no more war!

Nathan Miles (10)
Woodlands Primary School

Litter

If we recycle more we won't have rubbish on the roads.
Because if we didn't have recycling
There would be big amounts of rubbish everywhere,
But if we recycle we won't have rubbish everywhere.

Millie Clarke (9)
Woodlands Primary School